TRAINING TO SUCCEED

Cricket

Edward Way

FRANKLIN WATTS
LONDON • SYDNEY

First published in 2009 by
Franklin Watts
338 Euston Road
London NW1 3BH

Franklin Watts Australia
Level 17/207 Kent Street
Sydney NSW 2000

Words in **bold** are in the glossary on page 31.

Series editor: Sarah Peutrill
Art director: Jonathan Hair

Series designed and created for Franklin Watts by Storeybooks.
Designer: Rita Storey
Editor: Nicola Edwards
Photography: Tudor Photography, Banbury (unless otherwise stated)

Picture credits
© 2003 Getty Images p7, © 2006 Getty Images p27, © 2007 Getty Images p26. Every attempt has been made to clear copyright. Should there be any inadvertent omission please apply to the publisher for rectification.

Thanks to Sam and Woody of the JW Cricket Academy for all their help and to Bradfield College for the use of their facilities. Also thanks to Hamza, Tom and Freddie for their participation in the book.

A CIP catalogue record for this book is available from the British Library.

Dewey classification: 796.358
ISBN: 978 0 7496 8498 3

Printed in China

Franklin Watts is a division of Hachette Children's Books, an Hachette UK company.
www.hachettelivre.co.uk

Contents

Me and my sport

Cricket is an exciting, involving team sport for eleven players a side. It calls on a range of different skills: the batting team tries to score as many runs as possible while the fielding team aims to stop the batting side scoring runs and to take wickets to get the batting players out.

Cricket can be played for fun in or out of school, at clubs and in casual matches in parks. Some talented young cricketers want to take their interest further. They hope to make it into the professional ranks where they will be paid to play cricket as their career. In this book, three cricketers and their coach will share their experiences of training and performing with you.

All three cricketers hope to compete at the highest level. It will take skill, dedication, passion and a degree of luck to make the grade.

First-class cricket

First-class cricket is the highest level of cricket played within a country, such as County Championship games in the UK or Pura Cup matches in Australia. First-class matches usually last for three or more days.

Hamza Riazuddin

Hamza is 18 years old and has just left school. He is an **all-rounder**, which means that he is skilled at bowling and batting. He bats and bowls right-handed. He made his first-class debut for Hampshire versus Somerset in May 2008 and his first **Twenty20** appearance for Hampshire a month later.

My hobbies include playing other sports such as football and hockey. I also have a close interest in music and fashion.

Cricket has a mental edge over all the other sports in my opinion. A batsman has to concentrate for long periods of time and although it may not be as physically enduring as football, for example, there are many other aspects of it tactically and emotionally that are unique.

Freddie Walker

Freddie has just turned 17 and is studying for A levels at school. He is a batsman who has had trials with Hampshire and Gloucester county cricket clubs. He is working hard towards breaking into a first-class county in Britain.

I enjoy playing football and hockey as well as cricket. When we first played cricket, my older brothers Charlie and William wanted to bowl, which forced me to bat. But I liked it from the first time I picked up the bat.

Tom Jewell

Tom came through Surrey County Cricket Club (CCC) Academy where he was their Player of the Year in 2007. He is an all-rounder who made his first class debut in 2008 for Surrey versus Loughborough University.

I am 17 years old and I'm in year 13 at school. I enjoy socialising with my mates from school when not playing cricket and enjoy watching all sports. I spend a lot of time with my girlfriend. I have a big interest in cars as well.

*This batsman is out as the ball has hit his **stumps** and knocked off the **bails**.*

Starting out

People are motivated to play cricket for different reasons. Sometimes, they first learn from their family or are inspired by watching a match on television. Their early steps into the sport can be crucial.

I started to play cricket at a young age through the influence of my dad really. He played a lot of cricket and I would always follow him to his games. I guess my true passion for the sport started there.

I first played on a tennis court with my two older brothers, then at school when I was seven years old. My family encouraged me but I also wanted to play.

I first watched a cricket match on TV showing the under 21 England team play. That really inspired me as a seven year old to take up the game.

Kabir Ali of England shows young players how to bowl during a Kwik Cricket lesson in Kennington, London.

Starting out schemes

Many countries run special cut-down versions of the game suitable for young players who are just starting out. These include Kwik Cricket for 5-11 year olds and Inter Cricket for 12-14s in the UK and Milo Have-A-Go and Have-A-Game schemes for children up to the age of 12 in Australia. Summer camps such as the **MCC**'s Spirit of Cricket Challenge also exist.

Many schools and cricket clubs run cricket teams for young players and this remains the

At the under 13 regional festival at Taunton I felt that yes, I could do this at the very top level. It was the opening match of the tournament bringing together the best 44 players in my age around the country. I scored 108 not out and took 2 wickets for 3 runs. I was also captain and we won.

most common way for players to get a taste of a competitive cricket match.

These are usually age-banded which means that as players get older or better they move up to an older team.

My club cricket continued at Mortimer West End and I managed to break into the under 15 team at the age of 11 and the Berkshire under 11 county team at the age of 10. My cricket just started to become serious. I worked very hard at my bowling mainly because I had a real passion for it.

In competition

As the most talented young players progress, they may get selected for regional teams or play in tournaments against other young players. There, they get the chance to pit their skills against better players. If successful, like Hamza, it may start them thinking about taking cricket seriously as a potential career.

Cricket is a fast and sometimes dangerous game. Cricketers use protective equipment to guard against injuries.

In training

To improve as players, cricketers train frequently under the eye of a coach. Their training is split up into different elements – working on techniques, on general fitness and on match situations.

Fitness first

In general, cricketers need quick acceleration and good fitness levels to keep focused throughout a long match. Some of these targets can be reached through running and swimming and by working in the gym to strengthen muscles.

*My training session would usually include 30 minutes' bowling, a 20 minute bat against bowlers, 30 minutes on batting drills either on a bowling machine or with **throw downs** (when a coach tosses the ball to the batsman) and at least 10 minutes on fielding. I will also undergo a fitness programme that stretches through from the start of November all the way till the end of the summer… I feel in order to become a world class player you must put in long hard hours in the nets and in the gym.*

I train six days a week and I train for between 1 and 1½ hours. I warm up with a jog or maybe a little game of catch, and hit the stump. I then bat and bowl then get on the gym machines with my coach Julian Wood to warm down and finally, relax. Training's important because it helps me find out if some part of my game needs working on or why something went wrong in the last match.

This catching drill helps build sharp reactions. The players' coach hits the ball from close range giving the cricketer little time so that he has to make the catch quickly.

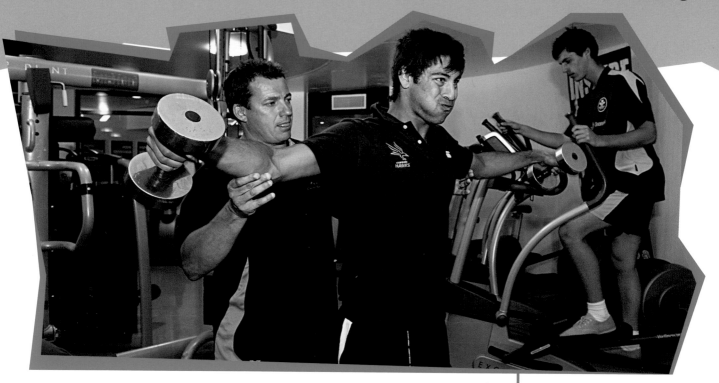

Tom, Freddie and Hamza's coach is Julian Wood (see page 11). He says, "There is a lot of focus on fitness, flexibility, speed and general awareness so that the players know most about their bodies."

Once into their teens, many cricketers work on strengthening key muscles in the gym. This work is best carried out under a coach's supervision.

The season and off-season

A cricketer's year is split into two parts – the season when matches are played and the off-season during winter. Cricket training continues in the off-season for the most dedicated players.

In the early parts of the cricket year during winter my priorities will lie in technique where I will target certain parts of my bowling action or batting to improve. During winter, I will be training pretty much four to five times a week for around an hour each time. However once the season commences and you find you are playing three games a week, it is hard to keep on training at such high intensities so frequently.

Coach's notes: flexibility

Flexibility exercises help increase a person's range of movement, which is how much they can bend their arms, back and legs without injuring themselves. Flexibility is especially important for bowlers who put great strain on their bodies but is useful in fielding and batting as well.

Working with my coach

The coach is one of the most important people in a young cricketer's life. Coaches form a strong bond with their players as they improve their skills, motivation and preparation to play cricket.

Meet the coach: Julian Wood

Julian represented England Under 15s and Under 19s and went on to become a professional player for Hampshire and a successful player-coach for both Newcastle Districts in Australia and Amanzimtoti Natal in South Africa. Captain of Berkshire CCC for seven years, he is the cricket professional at Bradfield College and became Director and Head Coach of the JW Cricket Academy in 2005. The people he coaches call him 'Woody'.

Julian Wood

The role of a coach

Coaches have to perform a number of different roles. A good coach can spot the potential in a player and then work with them to make them as good a cricketer as possible. This will involve lots of drills and exercises to improve parts of their skills as well as analysis of their batting, bowling and fielding techniques, sometimes using video cameras and computers.

My dad recognised that I needed some sort of coaching and guidance as he had no idea of cricket. So once a week, I went to Woody's sessions and learnt more than anything at that very young stage the need to have motivation and drive. He inspired a passion in me about the game that I still feel today.

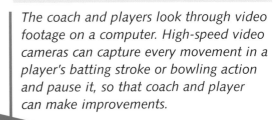

The coach and players look through video footage on a computer. High-speed video cameras can capture every movement in a player's batting stroke or bowling action and pause it, so that coach and player can make improvements.

The coach works with the batsman on his backlift (when he takes the bat back and up before bringing it down to play a shot). A coach can spot a tiny flaw which, if corrected, can make a big difference.

In the earlier stages of the academy when I was around 13 or 14, video footage was used thoroughly to highlight areas in my technique that either were in a good position or where improvements could be made…As a motivator Woody has been brilliant. To have someone constantly pushing you along and driving you to get more and more runs and wickets is priceless.

Woody is funny and lighthearted but he'll let you know if you're doing something wrong. He shows us where we're going wrong, for example, about footwork when batting. He helps with the mental side too, but he leaves it to you to fine tune it – like before you go out to bat he'll ask you what you're going to do against a certain bowler.

Different players need different assistance and experienced coaches adjust their coaching to suit each player. Sometimes, a player needs help with the mental side of cricket, learning ways of playing in certain situations, how to concentrate better and building their confidence.

Coach's notes: making decisions

Cricket is all about making the right decisions during a game. This only comes with experience and learning from your coach or coaches. Note down their advice in a training or match diary so you can refer to it later.

11

Working on batting

Every member of a cricket team needs to be able to bat well. Even as a tailender (a less capable batsman usually in the side as a bowler), a player can score valuable runs for the team which can turn a game from likely defeat to victory. If their batting improves considerably, they may be moved up the order which means they bat earlier in the innings.

Different strokes

Batsmen learn to be balanced as they face the bowling with their head up watching the ball as it leaves the bowler's hand. They need quick reactions either to leave the ball or to get into position to pick the right shot or stroke to play. They base their decision on the ball's pace (speed), its direction and whether it has swung in the air or changed angle when it lands on the pitch.

Woody really helped me to improve my batting technique. My role in cricket started to change and I entered the under 13 Berkshire team as an all-rounder, opening the bowling and the batting. I managed to take opportunities well with my batting, scoring runs at important times.

*I like the **pull** and the **drive** strokes. I like to attack the ball at all times. My favourite shot is the drive because it looks such a good shot when you get it right.*

The pull shot is an attacking stroke played to a ball pitched short but not rising much above waist height. The player swivels round to hit the ball, rolling his wrists to angle the bat down to keep the ball down.

*In the winter I will use the bowling machine to highlight a certain shot. For example, this year I used it to work on my horizontal bat shots such as the **sweep** and pull shot. It can help a lot in grooving a swing and building muscle memory.*

A bowler's big runs
Australian bowler and tailender batsman, Jason Gillespie scored an incredible 201 runs not out against Bangladesh in a 2006 Test Match.

Batsmen have to mix attack with defence to avoid getting out and learn a number of different shots through repetitive practice. All batsmen have their favourite shots but work very hard on shots they have yet to master. The more shots batsmen can play, the more tools they have to deal with balls reaching them at different heights, directions and speeds. Choosing the right shot to play can be tough and only comes with lots of practice and experience.

Training techniques

Cricketers mainly work on their shots either out on a field with a coach or another player throwing a ball to them or in the cricket nets. These are corridors of netting which allow batsmen to play their shots safely. The ball can be delivered by bowlers bowling or by using a bowling machine.

A bowling machine sends the ball towards the batsman at a set speed and lands it in the same place. This is helpful to let a batsman practise the same shot again and again.

This cricketer plays a backwards defensive shot. This shot plays the ball back straight and down. See how the player and his bat are in line with the ball.

13

Bowling training

Bowlers have two key aims: to stop the opposing batsman scoring runs and, most importantly, to get the opposing batsman out. They achieve this through unerring accuracy and knowledge of a batsman's weaknesses. They may also surprise a batsman by bowling a slower, faster or different angled ball to help force the batsman into making a mistake. Bowlers are sometimes helped by team-mates making brilliant stops or catches.

*Accuracy in terms of **line** and **length** is no doubt the most important aspect for a fast bowler. Over the past few months this has been hammered into my bowling regime. If I want to play at the top level I must build up the ability to bowl a ball in the same area over and over again.*

Grooving your bowling action

Bowlers practise all aspects of their bowling action frequently from their run-up to their follow-through and with their coach watching and providing tips. The aim is to groove their action so that they can repeat it again and again. Consistency and accuracy are key targets.

Hamza follows through after bowling the ball. A bowler's action should be smooth and have rhythm from the start of the run-up right through to the follow-through.

Hamza has a braced front leg as he brings his arm over to bowl. Bowlers practise their bowling in cricket nets either against a batsman or aiming for the ball to pitch in a small area to build their accuracy.

Julian takes Hamza through a drill where he is bowling the ball down a narrow lane marked out with cones. This target bowling drill helps a bowler work on the line and length of the balls he bowls.

Types of bowling

Bowlers often specialise in a certain type of bowling. Some tall and agile bowlers rely on the pace at which they can bowl the ball to trouble the batsman. Other bowlers strive to make the ball move sideways in the air (called **swing bowling**) or move sideways when it hits the pitch (**seam bowling**). Finally, there are several different types of **spin bowling** where the bowler puts spin on the ball so that it loops or dips during its flight through the air and moves off the pitch when it lands.

I'm a left arm medium pace bowler. As I'm coming in to bowl, I am thinking about where to pitch the ball. If I get hit for a big shot, though, I think about how fast I can get the ball down the other end!

Different ways of bowling the ball require different grips. Here, you can see a typical grip for a seam bowler (left) and a **leg-spin bowler**.

Fielding

Whilst one member of a team bowls, the other ten cricketers are in different positions around the ground to stop runs and possibly to take a wicket by catching the ball or running out a batsman.

Fielding positions

There are a large number of potential different fielding positions and a team's captain decides where to place fielders and picks team-mates based on their abilities. Some cricketers are great close catchers with sharp reactions and may stand in the **slips**, hoping to catch the ball if it deflects off the batsman's bat. Others who can throw the ball over long distances will field nearer the **boundary**, known as in the deep. See page 30 for all the fielding positions.

*My favourite position is **deep cover** or **mid wicket** when a spinner is bowling, as the ball comes towards me regularly and I feel I'm always in the game. I will generally work on close fielding such as making direct hits or diving catches to the left and right to simulate what a fielder in the extra cover or mid wicket position may receive.*

*My favourite fielding position is slip as it gives you a chance to get in the game more. I also field at **mid-on** and at **point**. We practise fielding at the end of every training session.*

Tom watches the ball right into his hands to take a high catch. As the ball reaches his hands he cushions the impact by bringing his hands down and in towards his body.

Fielding drills

Players perform many fielding and catching drills with their coach. Common catching practices include running and catching high balls and close catching practices (see picture above). Fielding practices often focus on stopping and picking up the ball cleanly and returning the ball accurately with a good throw.

Hamza sprints, collects the ball and returns it quickly to Tom who is backing up (standing behind the stumps). This sort of drill helps sharpen players' fielding and reactions and can lead to running out an opponent in a match.

I normally field in the slips or gully. Fielding is so important, you can save runs and turn games around with brilliant catches plus it sets a positive mood to the bowlers as well. I remember taking a diving catch in the gully last year playing against Somerset which was pretty special, diving to my right and managing to hold on. It is a pretty horrible feeling when dropping a catch. You just want to hide from everyone and run away.

Coach's notes: fielding

Fielding is so important as it enables you to contribute to the team, allows you to influence the game and takes pressure off the other disciplines (bowling and batting). In tight games where margins of victory are small, good fielding wins matches.

Tom makes a sliding stop to prevent the ball from reaching the boundary and the other team scoring four runs. He will need to get to his feet quickly and throw the ball back in accurately.

Setbacks and sacrifices

Young cricketers have to make sacrifices and can suffer setbacks during their career. Major setbacks might be a difficult injury, a loss of form with the bat or ball, or struggling with their form after moving to a new team. How players overcome these sorts of setbacks can determine whether they will progress and become professional cricketers.

A healthy diet

Cricket is an athletic sport so players need to eat healthily to fuel their activity. Coaches sometimes advise players on what to eat but it is the players' responsibility to look after themselves by eating healthy meals such as those containing lots of fresh vegetables and chicken, fish or lean meats.

Your diet is very important as a cricketer. I have recently learnt that I must eat a lot more as my workload can be quite significant as a bowling all-rounder. I think proteins are crucial in building and repairing muscle but also having a large breakfast is fundamental. I think if you eat well six days a week you can treat yourself to treats on the seventh but I generally do stay away from the fast food restaurant.

Being injured when I was 15 (it wiped out half my season and nearly a whole winter) was probably my lowest point. I had to go on a training rehab programme which was pretty intensive work and lengthy. It was very frustrating not being able to join my team-mates and play. I've never felt like giving up, but there have been moments when I've needed a break from the game to refresh my energy for playing and create that hunger to play.

Fresh fruit is one of a range of healthy snacks cricketers eat during the day.

Missing out?

There are lots of tasty yet healthy meals so eating responsibly does not need to be a sacrifice. Missing out on leisure time with friends can be more of a burden.

I guess in the short term you feel you do miss out on quite a bit. There have been loads of times when I haven't been able to go out with mates because I have cricket the next day. But I tend to look at the bigger picture, realising that to be a professional you have to dedicate a lot of time and effort. The reward of being a professional sportsman is definitely worth the effort and frustration you may have as a teenager.

Coach's notes: eat well

Stay away from stodgy foods; these can make you feel lethargic and tired. Eat lots of fruit, vegetables and pasta and drink lots of water especially when in hot climates. Whilst playing, jelly babies, Jaffa cakes and similar are good for instant energy.

Throughout setbacks, a cricketer's coach can help motivate and help a player work out what is going wrong and help to put it right.

Big match preparation

To perform at their peak, players have to prepare thoroughly before a big match. This involves a mixture of physical exercises to get the body warmed up and loosened up. It also involves getting the mind focused so that the cricketer is completely ready to play.

*I make sure I have a good bowl in the middle from both ends. In terms of batting, I would have 10 to 15 minutes of throws simply hitting **drive shots** with my bat using a strong top hand. Included in this I will have some underarm feeds for some **cuts** and pulls.*

Normally, we would turn up to the game an hour and a half before the start of the game. A dynamic warm-up would be the first thing to take place, this would be done as a team, loosening all the major muscles. After that, fielding drills would commence. These consist of high and low catches and ground fielding plus the slip fielders would practise taking nicks off the bat. After the fielding practices, the players separate and either have a practice bowl or receive throw downs to practise batting.

The cricketers perform a sharp fielding drill; collecting the ball and throwing it back accurately.

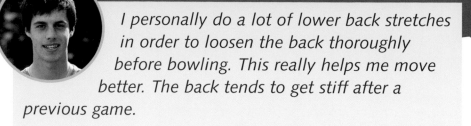

I personally do a lot of lower back stretches in order to loosen the back thoroughly before bowling. This really helps me move better. The back tends to get stiff after a previous game.

Hamza performs a stretch which will loosen his hamstrings (the tendons that run down the back of the upper leg).

Freddie stretches his arm and shoulder muscles with this exercise.

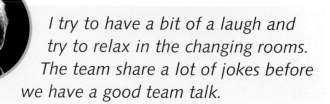

I try to have a bit of a laugh and try to relax in the changing rooms. The team share a lot of jokes before we have a good team talk.

Stretches

After some light exercise such as jogging, cricketers stretch all their key muscle groups in their legs, arms, back and neck. This helps get them ready for the exertion ahead and also helps prevent injury. Some players pay particular focus to an area of their body with which they have had problems in the past.

Mental preparation

After the warm-up, stretching and any drills and practice, the players regroup in their changing room. Players listen to team talks from their captain and coach and try hard to banish any nerves they may feel.

The players examine the pitch closely. Different pitches vary and may suit particular bowlers or batsman a little more.

In competition

Once the match starts, players have to be switched on, ready to react to whatever happens. For the batsmen waiting to bat, it can be a nerve-wracking time. But good players learn to stay calm whilst waiting for their turn to go out and bat.

Out in the field

A cricket team can be fielding for many hours at a time, yet fielders need to stay sharp and alert for the ball coming their way. Many players choose to switch off from concentrating in between deliveries.

Waiting to bat makes me more nervous than opening the batting but I do keep on watching the game and have the odd throw down to keep ready.

In the field and when batting you don't need to be focused after the ball's been bowled. I try and have a few seconds to relax, then switch back on again for the next ball. In the field there is a lot of noise as we all get behind each other.

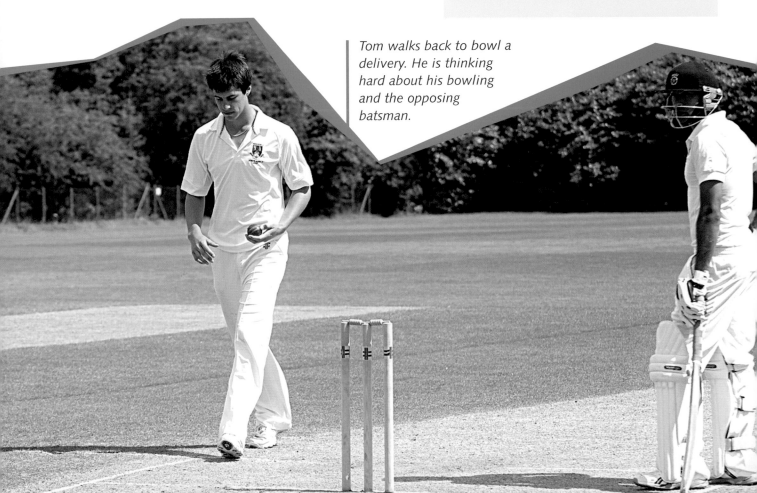

Tom walks back to bowl a delivery. He is thinking hard about his bowling and the opposing batsman.

Sharp, alert fielding means that Tom receives the ball and hits the stumps with it to run out an opposing batsman.

Under pressure

During a match, a team or individual can find themselves under pressure. It might be when batting with just a few runs required to win or bowling when the opponents are batting comfortably and scoring lots of runs. Good young players need the confidence not to let a tough situation affect their performance.

I am the type of guy who enjoys the pressure of competition. If my team is doing badly I always feel that I can make the difference and change the game round to our advantage. I raise my game when against tougher competition. This doesn't mean I try any harder but I feel when the pressure is on, I cope with it better than others.

I don't tend to get that nervous before batting, but get more nervous when bowling. I feel that I am quite a relaxed player when batting or bowling. I don't really get too angry or frustrated.

Building experience

When a match ends, the players warm down, shower and change. Later, they will reflect on how the game went and how they played as individuals within their team. All cricketers experience bad games as well as good ones. The secret is to learn from all performances to build experience and improve as a player.

*In my first game last year, out of our total of 183 runs I scored 103 not out and then bowled five **overs** and took 3 for 18. One that didn't go well was a Twenty20 final where I only scored 20 and then bowled and got "carted" (hit for runs frequently).*

Playing the pro's

As Tom, Freddie and Hamza progress, they will come up against adult professional cricketers with far more experience than themselves. Some of these encounters may lead to defeat or a poor individual performance, yet a young cricketer can learn much from these tests.

When bowling at pro's at a young age you realise quickly that the margin for error is so much smaller than when bowling at people of my own age. To experience bowling against pro's you learn lots very quickly.

*Freddie sways out of the line of a **bouncer**. Batsmen may have to endure a tough time for a period when the bowlers are on top. It's very satisfying for batsmen to get through this difficult spell without losing their wicket and then score plenty of runs afterwards.*

Analysing performance

A coach often talks to players as a complete team after a match, running through important points that come out of the match. Individual cricketers spend time thinking about how they played and may seek out their coach or team-mates for advice. Poor performances can be troubling but young players try to take positives and lessons without worrying so much that they lose confidence in their abilities.

Coach's notes: learning from a game

After you've fully recovered from a game, think carefully about how it went and how you played. Note down which aspects you could improve on and aim to work hard on them in training.

After a game of cricket, I will analyse my performance by writing in my internet diary about what went right and wrong. I will rate myself out of 10 for all three areas of the game and comment on anything I should do before the next game that could help me play better. Having my coach talk through my performance after a game can be very good. There are times when you can tend to forget areas where you have been good or even not so good that the coach can pick up on.

Many players find talking over the events in a game with a good friend in their team helpful. Others prefer to spend time alone carefully running through their performance and thinking about where improvements could be made.

Our heroes

Somerset batsman Marcus Trescothick sweeps a ball to the boundary during the Friends Provident match between Somerset and Sussex at Taunton in 2007.

Every spectator has his or her own heroes but people sometimes forget that sportsmen and women also may have people they admire. Sometimes, a cricketer's hero is someone who has won major competitions and set major records such as Brian Lara's world record 400 runs in a single Test match innings.

Some cricketers become heroes because of the way they play the game, their particular skills with the bat, ball or in the field or their attitude and approach to each cricket match. Young players may not be able to copy the precise bowling actions or strokes of their heroes, but they can learn a lot from watching their favourite players in action, live and on television.

My first hero was Marcus Trescothick. He was the very first left-handed batsman I saw on TV and I liked the way he batted. I meet my hero every day because he is my cricket coach, Julian Wood! I admire him because of his love of the game and how he wants everyone to play and do well in it. I don't try to copy his technique so much, but I do try to follow the wanting to do well every time I bat and his love for the game.

I can't really say I grew up with a cricketing hero. There was no one in particular that I personally admired. I think I just enjoy watching the game as a whole.

*Kevin Pietersen of England pulls a delivery from Brett Lee of Australia during an **Ashes** Test Match.*

The players I look up to now the most have to be Kevin Pietersen and Brett Lee. Brett Lee for me is the perfect cricketer in terms of image. He runs in hard and fast all day long for his team with a smile on his face. He plays with passion and grit but is a very humble performer.

I admire Pietersen because of his confidence and guts. He is a man who backs himself 100%. I was fortunate to play with KP in my first class debut at the start of this season. Of course, I was very nervous, but after the first few sessions of cricket I got to know him quite well. We got on well and I got to see not only the fun side of him on the field but his outstanding professionalism in preparation and concentration.

Taking the next step

Successful young cricketers like Freddie, Hamza and Tom cannot rest on their laurels. They have to continue to work hard to progress and improve. Players along with their coach will set a range of targets. Some might be fitness-based, such as increasing their fielding speed and sharpness. Others will be skills-based, such as mastering a particular shot or bowling a certain type of delivery.

Career goals

Players set goals for themselves to achieve in their career, such as breaking into a state side in Australia or playing in top class One Day or Twenty20 matches. Once in a side, they will have to continue to work hard to stay in it and become a regular member. Sometimes, players need that little bit of luck to get the opportunity in the first place.

My goal is to be the best batsman I can be and to play for a major county. I want to train with them and show their coach how well I can play so that they'll give me a chance in a match.

I feel the next major goal for me as a cricketer is to sign a professional contract with Surrey County Cricket Club and to secure a long career in the game.

My next goal is to become a regular player in the Hampshire one day squad as a genuine all-rounder. If all goes well in cricket I would like to say at 23 years of age that I am playing for England in one day internationals and have broken through into the Test Match side.

Paid to play

Cricket clothing and equipment can be expensive, so sponsorship deals where a company gives talented young players free clothing, equipment and sometimes a fee can really help. At the highest level, cricketers playing for their national teams and in competitions such as the Indian Premier League can become wealthy.

Cricket does not pay as well as football but I love the game. The equipment does cost a lot – up to £300 for a top-of-the-range bat – which is a lot more than a pair of football boots.

The monetary rewards, now with the introduction of Twenty20 cricket and the IPL leagues, are outrageously high. For a young man wanting to be successful and financially secure, cricket could not be any more appealing than right now. But this does not outweigh the feeling of playing for your country or representing a team that goes on to win the Friends Provident County Final or scoring a hundred in front of a massive crowd against a rival team. It is these things, not money, that attract me most and make all the sacrifices worthwhile.

Glossary

all-rounder A player skilled at both batting and bowling in a cricket team.

Ashes A bi-annual cricket tournament, played between teams from England and Australia.

bails The two wooden cylinders placed on top of the three stumps to form the wicket.

bouncer A short-pitched delivery bowled by a bowler that rises up towards the batsman's chest or head.

boundary The edge of the cricket field marked by a rope. If the ball is hit and crosses the rope the batsman scores four runs (or six runs if it hasn't bounced before crossing the rope).

cut A type of cricket shot hit with a horizontal bat usually to a ball well outside off-stump.

drive A type of cricket shot hit forward with a straight bat.

innings The period in which one side bats.

leg-spin bowler A right-handed bowler who spins the ball using the wrist to make the ball turn from right to left after it lands.

length A term used to describe how far up the pitch a delivery lands after leaving the bowler's hand.

line The direction in which the ball travels after leaving the bowler's hand.

MCC Short for the Marylebone Cricket Club which was founded in the 18th Century and is based at Lord's cricket ground in London.

off-spin bowler A right-handed bowler who spins the ball using the fingers, making it move from left to right when it lands.

over The division of play during which six balls are bowled at the batsman by a single bowler.

pull A type of shot played by swinging the bat in front of the body and hitting the ball to the leg side.

run The basic unit of scoring.

seam bowling A type of bowling where the bowler aims to get the ball to bounce sideways off its seam when it lands.

slips Fielding positions placed to one side of the wicket-keeper with the aim of catching a ball that is edged off the bat.

spin bowling A type of bowling where the bowler adds spin to the ball with the fingers or wrist to make it turn or deviate sideways when it lands.

stumps The three vertical poles of wood at each end of a cricket pitch.

sweep A type of shot where the ball is swept around behind the batsman with the batsman's back knee very low or touching the ground.

swing bowling A type of bowling where the bowler aims to get the ball to curve through the air.

Test match The highest form of cricket with national teams playing matches lasting two innings each for a maximum of five days' play.

throw downs A form of batting practice where a coach or another player throws the ball to pitch near the batsman from a relatively short distance away.

Twenty20 A new format of cricket which each team plays for a maximum of 20 overs per side.

wicket The arrangement of stumps and bails at one end of the pitch.

Fielding positions

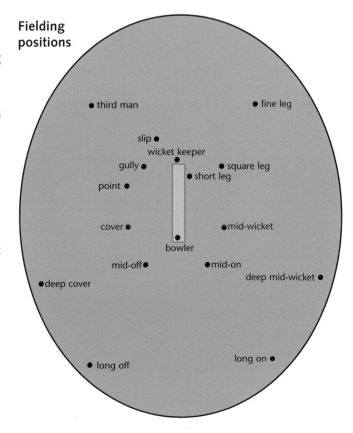

Find out more about cricket

Books

Know Your Sport: Cricket – Chris Oxlade (Franklin Watts, 2006)
A comprehensive guide containing everything you need to know to enjoy cricket.

Young Wisden: A New Fan's Guide to Cricket – Tim De Lisle (A&C Black, 2007)
An attractive and informative guide to cricket for the beginner.

Teach Yourself Cricket - Mark Butcher and Paul Abraham (Teach Yourself Books, 2007)
A useful book giving advice on batting, bowling, fielding, training and captaincy.

SAQ Cricket: Speed, Agility and Quickness For Cricket – Alan Pearson (A&C Black, 2004)
Although training is best carried out hands-on with a cricket coach, this book is an excellent guide to the sort of training cricketers can perform while away from their coach to improve their overall fitness and speed.

Websites and DVDs

www.lords.org/laws-and-spirit/laws-of-cricket
Knowing the Laws of Cricket well is an essential part of improving as a cricketer. They are available to read free at the official website of Lord's cricket ground.

www.ecb.co.uk/development
The development section of the England and Wales Cricket Board's website contains lots of information on coaching, club access and other ways to play and enjoy cricket.

http://cricket.com.au
The official website of Cricket Australia is large and contains pages on schools and local club cricket as well as training schemes.

www.blackcaps.co.nz
The official website of New Zealand's cricket team, the Black Caps.

http://news.bbc.co.uk/sport1/hi/cricket/skills/default.stm
The BBC cricket site has lots of tips on various aspects of playing cricket including video masterclasses on spin bowling from Australian coach, Terry Jenner and throwing from Paul Collingwood.

www.cricinfo.com
Get all the latest news, statistics and facts on your favourite cricketers and teams at the biggest cricket information website.

www.fitness4cricket.com
Learn more about injuries, recovery, getting fit and keeping fit as a cricketer at this website.

www.jwcricketacademy.co.uk
The homepage of Julian Wood's Cricket Academy where the three young cricketers featured in this book are coached.

Cricket: The Bob Woolmer Way (Green Umbrella Productions, 2007).
Featuring South African legends including Gary Kirsten and Jonty Rhodes, this is a high quality DVD guide to playing cricket by the former South African and Pakistan coach Bob Woolmer.

Note to parents and teachers: Every effort has been made by the Publishers to ensure that these websites are suitable for children, that they are of the highest educational value, and that they contain no inappropriate or offensive material. However, because of the nature of the Internet, it is impossible to guarantee that the contents of these sites will not be altered. We strongly advise that Internet access is supervised by a responsible adult.

Index